The Family Secret

JANICE FREEMAN

ISBN 978-1-967361-36-6 (Paperback)
ISBN 978-1-967361-37-3 (Ebook)

Inquiries and Book Orders should be addressed to:

Leavitt Peak Press
17901 Pioneer Blvd Ste L #298,
Artesia, California 90701
Phone #: 2092191548

Contents

Dedication

I wish to thank the Lord for encouraging me to write this book and all those who made it possible.

Acknowledgements

DEAR SISTERS IN THE LORD
Krystal, Marsha, Kea, Tracey

Introduction

Segregation has done terrible damage to the lives of African-Americans in our country since the beginning of slavery. This damage has been recorded, primarily as it affected the African- American community over the last 300 years.

The great mistreatment that this community suffered has been told through the late nineteenth and twentieth centuries. However, a story has also been told how segregation has damaged and demeaned white people who came to America. It changed many of them into extremely prejudiced people, using this prejudice to do terrible harm. If it was not for the Civil Rights Movement, this condition would still be going on today in the strength that it existed in the past. God in His mercy raised up men and women in these last 100 years who were African-American, white, and other nationalities who have resisted to the death this hateful bigotry.

A white family that also experienced this damaging movement through most of this segregation practiced in the nineteenth and twentieth centuries experienced the other side of how white people too were affected by this pernicious practice. They thought their actions were right, until great sacrifice on the part of the predominantly African-American community opened their eyes through the family's secret. This story is about that family.

Chapter 1

"THE FAMILY"

I am the second of two daughters, and in my particular family and in my lineage there were two judges, two senators, one admiral, and several West Point Graduates, all of whom were successful. Some are listed in the nation's history books. That's why I can't breathe the family's last name.

My name is MaryAnn and my sister's name is Clare. Both of us were born to a wonderful mother and father. My parents were from the Deep South and were wrapped up in all the traditions of the Deep South. Both of them were white, and were from wealthy families. Their heritage took them back to the early founding of the Southern states. They were very proud of that heritage and all of their family's achievements.

My mother was very beautiful and grew up in one of those old plantation homes, with all the finery and space that these homes could afford. She had a finishing school education and impeccable manners. When she reached eighteen she was sent to one of the finest white woman's Southern colleges. My father attended an outstanding college nearby. He also came from one of the finest Southern families and was raised with all the finest trappings that a gentleman from his background and wealth would need to have. He lived in a beautiful home with servants.

He was trained in all the fine skills that a man of his background should possess. This training was on a large plantation where there was hunting, fishing, agriculture, supported by share cropping and servants. When he reached his college years he was sent to one of the finest male colleges in the South.

I mentioned the beauty of my mother, but my father, was as handsome as she was beautiful. His father who was an outstanding business man wanted him trained in Liberal Arts because he had already learned a lot about business through his father's nurturing. Like my mother, he was very smart and excelled in his college work at every academic level. He also was outstanding in sports having learned sporting skills on the large plantation where he was raised. So whether it was sports or academics he was at the top of his game.

As I was told later in life when he saw and met my mother he was smitten and knew he would marry her. She arrived at her college two years after he came to his school and he was going into his junior year that fall. My mother sought a liberal arts degree because at that time wealthy young ladies wanted to be educated but did not plan to work but instead settle down into a good marriage. This is just what happened as planned by her family. The exception to this choice was to do volunteer work which she did through charities and the church. She felt this was her duty and she didn't seem to strive for more.

My parents attended the Southern Baptist Church and both of them sincerely believed in their Christian faith and doctrines and both had a genuine born again experience which they later shared with Clare and me.

My mother was a great reader, so those recommended books and expensive magazines kept her abreast of what was happening around the world. Because of his job my father was able to take her on trips to Europe, the Middle East, and the Far East, which was part of his business travel and vacation plans. My grandmother and grandfather loved it when both of us visited them. Staying with them was like moving into the same house as our own with all the same rules. The bigger thing they had in common with my parents was their great love for us. When our parents came home we were so happy to see them, along with the wonderful gifts they brought with them for us from abroad.

Chapter 2

"Moving North"

*W*hen I was five and my sister Clare was seven, my father was offered a position in the Northeast as the Head of a top Pharmaceutical company. He had been second in charge of his pharmaceutical company in the South. Not only had he brought a great amount of business into the company, but he was chosen to head this newly built northern company. He was a little apprehensive about fitting in to this new Northern environment knowing that his roots were deeply Southern. However he always had a laid back personality which made it so that he could adjust to change without frustration in most situations and without compromising what he believed was right. He like my mother was a reader and he acquainted himself with any area he was going to move to including its history and every nook and corner involving the population that he might be involved with. He also recognized that the South had its faults regarding the

Civil War even though his love of the South was as deep as those who fought in the Civil War.

The move went very smoothly and Clare and I were placed in a private Quaker school which was outstanding in academics, etiquette, and sports. Because of our prior Southern training we fit right in and were treated very well. Due to the size of the home it was easy for my mother to entertain the school's children and adults at parties. This endeared her to the school staff and they loved her southern accent. Both my mother and father liked the area they had picked for our new home and we did also.

Clare was truly a big sister and watched out for me wherever we went together. She was very feisty, lots of fun, and always top in her class. My parents put a lot of responsibility on her involving my care and I could say I was more spoiled than she because I was the baby girl. Clare didn't resent it but liked being in charge of me, and because of my personality I liked depending on her. My parents belonged to the country club in our community which consisted of the wealthiest residents and also represented a type of the life they were used to in the South.

The Quaker school we attended went from kindergarten to our senior year in high school. It was full of activities and special trips, to museums and listening to speeches from interesting people for our different age groups. School was pretty exciting. I can't even remember ever being bored and Clare fit in everywhere. She seemed to master everything. I was so very proud of her. I never felt jealous of any of her achievements.

Chapter 3

"OUR FRIEND JENIFER"

There were some African-American students in our school and now as I look back I realize that none of our teachers ever made a racial difference with these students. They were all treated equally. When I was 12 and Clare was 14, one of the African-American girls who was very smart became very close to Clare.

Their interests were the same and both of them seemed to love learning. They loved books and when projects were assigned, their projects seemed to be exceptional. One day Clare asked my mother if this girl whose name was Jenifer could come to the house after school and mother said she could. Clare never mentioned that she was African-American so when her mother brought her over, there at the door my mother invited both of them in to the vestibule. There they introduced themselves. I thought it was strange because my mother always invited those coming to visit into the house, mainly because those visiting admired so many things in our house especially items brought home from overseas trips. Of course these invitees were her white friends. Since they came at 4pm Jenifer's mother asked at what time she should come to pick her daughter up. My mother said that we usually had dinner at 6pm and realized it would only give both girls very little time together. She then said that Jenifer could eat with the family and they usually finished eating at 7:30pm. Both women agreed and Jenifer's mother left. My mother didn't realize I was in the next room when she called my father. Clare and Jenifer had gone upstairs to Clare's room. My mother was explaining that Jenifer was an African-American girl which Clare had never mentioned. Because of the liberal policies at the Quaker school Clare never thought of mentioning it.

My father who was now settled into his new job came in contact with different races. He seemed to take it in stride and mentioned that they would discuss the matter involving Jenifer when he came home. I found this out later when mother discussed the call with me. Also that evening when the girls were called down to dinner my mother was surprised that Jenifer's table manners were impeccable and whatever they discussed at the table she seemed to hold her own in the conversation. They also noticed how well she got a long with Clare and there was much chatter and laughing around the table. At the table, Mom and Dad learned that Jenifer's father was a dentist and her mother was the head nurse at one of the departments of a white hospital. My father was familiar with it because pharmaceuticals and medical supplies were part of his business.

Jenifer's mother came at 7:30pm and picked her up but she still was not invited into the house but waited in the vestibule. However, my father asked her to come in and along with my mother they chatted for a few moments and then she and Jenifer got in their car. After they left my mother and father spoke about how exceptional she was and he reminded my mother that many African-Americans in the North had very good positions of employment and had good salaries. Their communities were integrated and it wasn't strange that her mother was a head nurse at a white hospital. My mother asked him if Jenifer could come again and he agreed. So that year there were visits to the house, but my mother though very polite could never be completely at ease with Jenifer's mother. However, on school projects both parents worked very well together.

Soon Clare started going to Jenifer's house as often as Jenifer came to our house. Clare loved it there and began taking me with her. Jenifer had two younger brothers which my father questionedme and Clare about. We explained that they were much younger than Clare and me but were very much fun to be with.

Sometimes when Jenifer's father was home from his office he would take all of us to a large ice cream parlor where we could get whatever we wanted and this was great fun. Clare and I had other friends come home too, but Jenifer was her best friend and I felt the same way about her. Even though I was younger, she always seemed to be interested in what I was interested in and then it happened. Jenifer and Clare were now 16 and she accompanied us on special trips within the state and sometimes out of the state. They were usually trips to add to our learning that both my mother and father were interested in.

However by the end of Jenifer's 16th year, she became very ill with leukemia, and in time she had to be taken out of school. Her mother had to come home from work to care for her. My parents were good about taking us to visit her and my mother offered to go to their house to give her mother a break in caring for Jenifer. This brought both women closer. Their visits opened my mother up more and more to their family. She even went as far as giving Jenifer a birthday party at our house so her whole class could come. She had gifts for every student and wonderful entertainment. This made my mother so happy because she loved doing charitable things. Jenifer's mother came to help and broke down and cried when she saw her daughter who was so ill with leukemia enjoying her schoolmates and teachers so much. Jenifer had only a few more weeks to live so her church also gave a wonderful party for her and she invited our family.

Our family had never been in an African-American Baptist church before with gospel singing and wonderful preaching and testimonies. The church itself was very beautiful inside. The choir had on very attractive robes and the altar furniture was beautiful.

When we arrived home we all felt very lifted and had a genuine spiritual experience. We didn't realize that in three weeks our dear friendwould depart this life on her heavenly journey. When the time came, the funeral was at the church, but this time there was much weeping and mourning. The music and singing were very beautiful releasing a sadness which was pure grief. Even my mother and father had tears in their eyes and Clare and I were leaning on our parents in tears. Her brothers were weeping on their parents. Many of our classmates were there and they too were very sad.

Clare told my parents that she didn't think she could go back to school knowing Jenifer wasn't coming back. I was now fifteen and Clare was almost seventeen and we were now aware of the terrible segregation coming out of the South as we were experiencing scenes from the Civil Rights movement. We watched how many African-Americans were terribly mistreated and sensed that our parents did not want us to watch all this drama. They didn't want the love we had for our southern families and traditions to be diminished. They tried to explain to us that all Southerners were not like these people we were seeing on television. Clare and I realized that they knew it had some effect on us which they tried to protect us from. There was a softening with them but not enough to see things that we saw by going to school with different people some of whom were exceptional African-Americans.

Somehow Clare and I realized that our family would never fully accept integration and now that we were older we realized that when our feet went over the threshold of our home we knew we were in a different world. We also knew that in order not to break our parent's heart we could never let them know how much we disagreed with their feelings about the races.

Chapter 9

"School Days"

By watching television we were aware that we were living in two worlds and we tried to do this peaceably not wanting to wound either one of our parents. Once in a while they would mention Jenifer and her family but we never saw them moving closer to be a friend to other African-Americans. Jenifer's mother and father still reached out to us and asked us to share special occasions with them which were always fun. Jenifer's mother went back to work at the hospital and one thing my father did was to reach out to her giving her a very good position in his pharmaceutical company. It was an executive position and we found out later, not only did she take it but he was very pleased with her performance. In the South he had never worked with a well-educated African-American person so this was a new experience for him coming to the North. He also hired other African-Americans in his company as well.

Soon Clare was eighteen. Her graduation was with honors and the time for Clare to go to college had come. Our parents wanted her to attend our mother's alma mater and Clare with my parents agreed. From what both of us learned at our school, there were very outstanding schools in the area where we lived but to please mom and dad, Clare acquiesced and was accepted at our mother's alma mater. As in high school, she excelled and there were always special events surrounding her achievements which our family flew to. Clare came home during holidays and she visited Jenifer's family on these occasions. She also confided in Jenifer's mother things that she could never share with our own mother, especially about race and civil rights. My father would let me fly to Clare's school alone to see her when there were three-day holidays.

The school was beautiful, and being out of our house we could share so many things that we couldn't share with our parents. Clare dated at school and had many friends, but she found something lacking in the male students coming from these surrounding schools. Most of these young men were well mannered and they wanted a deeper relationship with her. They also came from very fine Southern families, and their families were very much like our family. Clare did not want to marry into that environment. When these young men wanted more, Clare very cleverly got out of these relationships. Then it happened. Clare met a young man who was very handsome and extremely smart. His name was Hugh Grant. He had transferred into the school that daddy had attended from a college in the Northeast because his family had moved back to the South. His new home in the South was a long distance from where he attended school so he could not go home often. His family had money, but was not as wealthy as our parents. He dressed well and seemed to have enough money to afford whatever was necessary at school. Whenever he called home the money came.

Coming from a top Northern college he was one of the top students in his classes which impressed Clare and the other students as well. I met him on several occasions visiting her and could understand why Clare was so attracted to him. He was excellent in sports, academics, and he even had a job, so he didn't have a lot of time for socializing. Clare knew that he liked her but he didn't seem to want the relationship to get deeper, although when they were together she always had a wonderful time. She told me she thought she was falling in love with him but she didn't want him to know it until he showed signs that he felt the same way about her.

Everyone in our immediate family were blondes with blue eyes and very fair and most of our family still living in the South were also fair and blonde with blue eyes. Clare was a gorgeous blonde, tall like my father and very shapely.

I was considered cute with dimples, blonde curls and slightly plump and was now 17. I was smart but not brilliant like my sister. I was also somewhat shy. I did not meet the man I later married until I got to college. He was from a well-to-do family and a very good husband, but he very much held my families Southern beliefs. However, as the years went by, these beliefs changed for the better and were definitely modified.

My frequent trips to see Clare which were often, allowed me to see that both Clare and Hugh were falling in love with each other. I often thought if they married what would their children look like because his hair was dark brown, his eyes were brown and his skin was slightly darker than ours. To look at him you never doubted that he was white, born from parents that had brown hair and brown eyes and skin not quite as fair as our family. He was only slightly darker than our family members, but he would never be thought of as anything but white. After they got much closer she even brought him home on several occasions, and our parents were very proud of her choice and seemed to like him very much. My father was impressed with the Northern school he had attended and of course attending the school in the South which my father had graduated from. He was a pre-med major which was also impressive to both my parents. They could tell that Clare really cared for him and he seemed to really care for her. He was a gentleman at all times which my father appreciated.

This went on and continued even when I joined Clare as a student attending our mother's school. I was now eighteen and she was twenty and had two more years to go before her graduation. As he and Clare got closer they both began to share their deeper feelings for each other and also what their parents were like.

It seemed as if Hugh's father was a white man who met his mother while they were both in the service while stationed in the Northeast.

She was very pretty and was a very light skinned African-American woman. His father was blonde and fair and a rugged type of guy. He fell in love with Hugh's mother's femininity and lady likeness. Also she was a very moral person and a church girl. When they got out of the service they married and moved to a Northern city knowing that their chances would be better for their marriage and their children when they began a family. Their names were Frank and June Grant. Looking at her you really could not tell her true nationality. She could have been Italian, Hawaiian or East Indian or any race of a very light complexion with Nordic features. Living in the North made it easier for them to live because there were so many nationalities. Having been in the service they both found very good jobs and lived very well. Hugh was born a year later and was a tough little boy from birth and very cute.

When he reached five his father enrolled him into school as a white child and he and his wife felt this would always give him the best chance for education and any advantages he would need in life. His father took him to the South to meet June's grandmother who raised her when she was little but they never discussed race around him until he reached his teens. They just casually mentioned that his grandmother was brown because she was of a mixed race. He saw her so seldom, when he was very young he never gave her color much thought, or even thought of himself in that way. Also it was never mentioned. So from kindergarten all the way through high school and half way through college he attended the best predominantly white schools until their move to the South. His mother's company had another company in the South, so she was able to receive all of the same benefits that her Northern company offered. There Hugh attended our father's school as a white student in his junior year. He fit in very well and no one thought of him other than white.

Being a Northerner what really stood out with him was the confidence that his father instilled in him. He was their only child so he was exposed to the best of everything. Horseback riding, football, chess, roller and ice skating, and hunting and fishing which he grew up doing with his father. His mother and father lived their life around him as a white couple, but they were a couple that treated everybody well without any prejudice. Therefore Hugh never grew up with a racist attitude and got along with all his school mates, bringing them home, taking them on trips with his family no matter what their economic or racial status was. Like his father, he was an all-around guy and was loved very much by his mother. His mother had a very good job which she planned to retire from and his father had a top management job in a very prestigious company. They all drove nice cars, lived in a lovely neighborhood and attended a predominantly white church in that neighborhood. However they were not pretentious in any way, and got along with everyone in their church. There were several minority couples there and their pastor encouraged this even as far as going out into African-American neighborhoods or other minority places inviting people to the church. Frank and June did not let him know of June's status. It was mainly because they did not want their son's education to be jeopardized in anyway. June knew how segregated education could do harm to someone who wanted to be accepted into those schools where all learning was available. However, while in the service she took courses offered and also went to night school while Hugh was growing up, and was able to attain her bachelor's degree.

Clare and Hugh finally decided to get married. So right after her graduation our parents gave her a beautiful wedding at our home and I was her matron of honor. Hugh's father came, but explained that his wife was not able to come because she was ill, but she sent Clare a beautiful gift. The illness I learned later was not a lie, because she had a chronic illness but was able to work. She just had to be very careful.

Clare got a very good job after college and she attended graduate school. She and Hugh got a small apartment near her job and her school. Hugh had gotten accepted into medical school after his graduation and Clare and I were there to congratulate him along with his proud parents.

By this time all the attitudes of our mother and father had been explained to Hugh and his family which they perfectly understood. So after the wedding there was very little reason for them to meet again but it was never the same with Clare, me, and his parents. I was close to each of them knowing his mother's situation. Because of the influence of our Quaker School's open-mindedness about race, neither Clare nor I were troubled about Hugh's mother's race. Even though, if our parents knew it would not be accepted. So, this was between my sister and I.

I waited to marry right after my graduation, and even today I'm still happily married to a wonderful man named Donald Ferris. Over the years, we had three children but I did not share with him the family secret.

Chapter 5

"MY BEAUTIFUL SISTER"

Clare continued in graduate school and Hugh finished medical school with his parents continuing to support him. Clare tried to visit our parents when she and Hugh could but sometimes she had to go alone because of Hugh's busy schedule. The good news was that Clare got pregnant after a year of marriage and both of them were ecstatic. The baby was beautiful. A little girl named "Carlee." She weighed nine pounds at birth, with light brown curly hair, and with Clare's beautiful blue eyes. I helped when I could while still going to night school and my father and mother helped Clare while she was finishing graduate school and with her and Hugh's housing. Hugh was very responsible and because he was so bright, he picked up work at his medical school helping out in one of the medical programs.

All was going well and Clare, Hugh the baby and I shared everything. I think Hugh liked having a sister (me) because he did not grow up with any siblings. Things went very well after graduation and a very excellent job came through for Clare, and Hugh continued on with his specialty in medical school. Our mother and father provided a nanny while Clare worked, and the nanny was very good with the baby. I loved babysitting too, but after I graduated and married I was not as available as I had been, but I made it my business to see my sister and her husband and the baby as often as I could.

Clare had moved up on her job and in a year's time she reached an executive position. My father was very proud hoping that Clare and Hugh would move north and she would join his company. After a year into working, Clare began to have female trouble and she realized something was wrong and went for tests. It was discovered that she had ovarian cancer which had never showed up in any previous exams but now that it had she was devastated.

Even in such a short time her company could see what an asset she was and didn't want to lose her. Hugh encouraged her to work part time as long as she felt up to it. Hugh researched every known cure and through his contacts he reached out to everyone he could for help with her illness. Our father, being in the pharmaceutical field contacted specialists also in and out of his pharmaceutical companies. Hugh cheered her up and even encouraged her to keep working which she did. Her busyness kept her active and not concentrating on her illness as much as she would have. However, by the middle of that next year when Carlee was two, Clare had to leave her job because there seemed to be little hope.

Clare went to our parent's home with Carlee to spend time with our parents and they could really see the toll that this illness had taken on her. Their beautiful tall girl (still beautiful) was now a size five and her long heavy hair was still blonde but had thinned out considerably. After she spent two weeks home she wanted to get back to Hugh, realizing they wouldn't have much time together. Hugh's mother felt so bad that she wanted to use the sick leave program her company offered to come and help Clare with the baby. So a week after Clare got home, June came and spent time with both of them. She stayed at a hotel and came very early and left late in the evening. She took Clare for rides, and to tourist areas, and to the children's parks with the baby, and Clare really enjoyed her time with her mother-in law. At the airport, tears came to Hugh's eyes as his mother left.

The time was now getting short so Clare and I talked about the baby. She later discussed these things with Hugh. She knew his mother couldn't leave her job to care for the baby because she had been there so long and would lose a large pension. She promised she would always look out for her in every way she could. It seemed like our mother and father were the only ones who could take her. Clare left little notes for Carlee telling her how much she loved her for her birthdays up until age 21. Clare asked me to lookout for Carlee which my husband and I tried to do throughout the following years.

Clare returned permanently to our home where she passed away. Clare's passing was very difficult for my mother, father, and Hugh mainly because she was young with such promise.

Hugh's mother came to the funeral, and my parents thought she was foreign but never African-American. It was too impolite of my parents to ask and strangely when they did ask my opinion I always pretended that I didn't notice. I didn't mention that my father and mother were Southern Baptist at a time when the Southern Baptist doctrine was part of the segregated teachings they grew up with in the South. It wasn't until many years later that this large Southern Baptist Denomination recognized their segregated teachings were wrong and discontinued their teachings in this area. This was very well received by many in the Christian community. When Clare and I were young we were in church every Sunday morning with our parents and together we did believe in Jesus as our Savior. We attended prayer meetings on Wednesday and other religious programs as they came up. So the church our parents attended in the North had no African-Americans in the congregation. It was nothing like Jenifer's African-American Baptist church which was wonderful.

My parents took excellent care of Carlee but did not put her in the Quaker school that Clare and I grew up in. They sensed that it was too liberal for their belief system but it was still considered academically one of the best.

Chapter 6

"THE SECRET"

Carlee was a good child and loved all of us in the family. I could see though that my mother was trying to deliberately raise her in her Southern mold as much as she could. Because she and my dad were living in the North there were some things both of them had to let go of in order to fit into the society they were now living in. Also, the Civil Rights movement was still going on.

My parents took Carlee South more often since my father had longer vacations, and introduced Carlee to famous Southern heroes and other patriotic Americans who had contributed to our Nation. It developed in her a love for history which made her knowledgeable of some African-American history as well, but not overwhelming so. Carlee also loved the sciences and excelled in them all the way through high school.

Since my mother had now lost Clare, she reached out to Jenifer's mother more. Though they did not socialize together they became genuine friends. Talking about Carlee would be like talking about Clare and me growing up with the exception of our Quaker education. Carlee made my parents very happy but she seemed to really want to please them even more than Clare and I did. Carlee's father visited when he could and wrote but after finally getting into his medical practice he married again and had more children. Carlee visited them but less often as she got older. He married a white woman who was blonde like Clare so Carlee fit right into that family. As my family grew Carlee grew, and before we knew it she was getting ready to go to college and was growing up as a lovely young woman. She was extremely smart like her mother and very cheerful.

She was so happy with my parents that she hardly questioned them about anything.

When she graduated magna cum laude and valedictorian of her class she had already been convinced to go to her mother's school in the South and she was ready. When she arrived there she met nice boys in her school area but when she reached her junior year she met her true love. His name was Joe West, and he was Southern like my father, holding on to the traditions he could but having to release others in order to make it successful in the business world. When he graduated he went into his father's business and he brought him along in a way that he became very successful.

Carlee waited until she graduated and then mom and dad gave her a big wedding like they did for Clare and me. She even wore Clare's gown to please my mother. Many of Joe's family came and got along wonderfully with our parents. Hugh and his whole family came to be with Carlee and they gave Carlee and Joe their Honeymoon trip to Europe. Carlee loved her father's family and since they were in the South where she was at school she visited them as often as she could and they all got even closer after she and Joe got married.

Two years into the marriage Carlee became pregnant. She and Joe were very happy and excited as the months progressed. They had the nursery beautifully decorated knowing it was going to be a girl. Because Joe was blonde and very fair, the baby arrived blond; but looked very much like Carlee. Her hair was blonde like her father instead of light brown like her mother. We don't know how Joe heard it but a nurse at the hospital where the baby was born mentioned that the beautiful blonde baby in the nursery that everyone was talking about had African-American blood in her because of a birth mark on the lower part of her back. They had named the baby Clare after my sister Clare. No one would ever have suspected it when looking at her. Where Joe was standing, the nurse could not see him from her vantage point. As soon as Carlee got home from the hospital she noticed that something was wrong with her husband and she called me to discuss it.

Almost a week went by and then she told me about the remark he had heard. He discussed it with one of his young doctor friends. His friend explained to him that through heredity, sometimes traits of other races in our family ancestry can show up after several generations. It doesn't always happen where it is visible and told him not to worry about it since the baby was so fair with blonde hair. What Carlee did not know was that Joe was from a very racist family and even though they were wealthy like her family they were very prejudice going back generations, and that unlike her family several members of his family had been Klansmen for several generations with sympathies still in that area.

There were a lot of secret stories told by his father to Joe that his father was privy to. He or his father never participated in this behavior but the generation preceding his father's generation had. Joe never doubted Carlee's faithfulness to him but after much discussing it, he realized that he could not have his legal child be African-American even if only a drop of African-American blood existed in her. He said he would cooperate with her in doing for the child what was necessary and if she didn't tell her grandparents the true reason for their divorce that he would never discuss it with those that were close to him.

He wanted Carlee to divorce him using the reason of irreconcilable differences and he would not challenge her on any issue they had previously discussed. Carlee agreed, always hoping he would change his mind but he became more distant with her and the baby but not mean. He was more like a person who was fond of you but not in love or wanting to be involved with you. She discussed the whole matter with me, and chose to come back home but did not share his true reason with mom and dad.

Because of Clare's death they were so glad to have her home again even though she went through a deep depression and sought help as encouraged by my parents. Her doctor was one of my father's older friends and Carlee loved him. He seemed to sense that this divorce was deeper than she wished to share with him. He also let her know that because she was so young she would have to let the relationship go and plan a new start in her life. He advised her not to get romantically involved right away, but take time to get over Joe because her love for him was very sincere and also because he was her first relationship.

The doctor knew through counseling with her that Joe had deeper problems that probably would never heal. He let her know not to put any blame on herself. She was mentally healthy and just had to start over as soon as possible especially since she had a grandmother who could help her with her child. Joe paid for a nanny and setup a trust fund that would see his daughter through her educational goals. There was hardly anything that ever came up so with her grandfather's help Carlee got back into school. She was totally innocent in the whole situation and made up her mind that she would not get involved with anyone until she knew in her heart that she was truly over Joe. Because she was a science major in college and took as many extra courses as she could in science, she chose the field of medical research and she was accepted at the best Northern medical college in her area. Like Clare she hit the courses running. I constantly cheered her on and like Clare she just excelled in every way. I was concerned because it was all work and no play and I knew that in time she would have to get a social life which would give her a break from her studies.

When Carlee was accepted to medical school, she had two advanced lab courses that she had also taken as part of her undergraduate work. Therefore, the next level of lab work was for a third year medical student, and she qualified for this even though she was now only in her freshman year of medical school. She loved school and soon met several students that she became friends with.

She talked to me about one medical student who had become very close to her as a friend named Walter, who was African-American and she had finally shared her story with him and he was glad. He knew something was psychologically wrong with her marriage to Joe, and it was good she was out of it.

His specialty was Neurological Psychology and he also wanted to take special courses in psychoanalysis. He was a couple of years ahead of Carlee in Medical school but because of his interest in her situation he tried to find extra time out of his busy schedule to spend with her. Carlee was very beautiful but because of his race he wouldn't even allow his emotions to go in that direction. It was especially because it was a time in history when African-Americans were identifying with their own race with great pride.

When he did date he usually dated very attractive smart African- American women. When he was with Carlee he kept her laughing knowing this was good and necessary for her well-being. His laughing kept her depression at bay. When she would go to her home in the evening she would be smiling over something he said or acted out during the day.

Chapter 7

"HEALING"

*W*alter came from a wealthy African-American family. His father was a NFL football player who was very famous. The medical school Walter attended was glad to have such a parent of one of their students. They were also very happy about Walter's academic achievements. Carlee had heard about some things he had excelled in at school and she was very proud of him. Like her mother Carlee was very good in all her academic courses so she could understand most subjects that Walter discussed with her. She also shared with him that her father was a doctor in the South and she only saw him several times a year.

At that time Carlee had no idea that her father was an African- American man. Because of the grandparents up-bringing of her she never even thought of marrying an African-American man. By the time Carlee was a teenager, my parents had to let go of some of their strict beliefs about race. However within the home environment there was not a lot of movement in this area. The household was made up of a white Southern family who had moved from the Deep South to the North. Having done this they had let go some of their ideas but not many. They were true Christians though and were kind to people, but they were in a church that supported their prejudiced ideas. Because Carlee had been raised in the North she had met African-Americans along the way and was very comfortable with them. She had never seen her grandparents mistreat African- Americans or hear them talk in a negative way about them.

Her influences from my parents were very subtle, so like Clare and me, she knew there was a line not to be crossed involving race in the home, unless it was school or job related. Because of June's influence, my father introduced some very good changes in his company and even received awards for some. So basically his company ran like any other large Northern company adopting most of the civil rights changes through the years. Both of my parents were now getting older and keeping up with a three year old was wonderful but not easy. It was good they had a nanny for walks in the park, playing on the gymnastics equipment at the playground, story time at the library, and other recreational activities offered by the community. Any medical issues like dental work, inoculations, and children's programs dealing with health, mother took care of those and loved it.

Mother did not look her age even though she and father were aging. Many times people took her to be an older mother rather than a grandmother and that boosted her ego. All during her marriage mother kept herself up. She was at the beauty parlor each week, and manicures and pedicures were every two weeks. Salon massages and aerobics three times a week. All of this kept her in great shape. My father use to comment about how attractive she was and how proud he was when he took her to different functions at his company. Of course this gave her more confidence.

I remember how my father, even when he was older was at the gym faithfully which kept him looking good still keeping a full head of mixed blonde hair. Sometimes Carlee would talk about school mentioning Walter who was African-American and what a good friend he was and the fact that his father was a NFL football player. Father was familiar with him. She also mentioned that Walter was into sports in high school and college and graduated fourth in his class from his undergraduate university. Walter was now close to graduation from medical school, and he had to get into his residency after graduation. He could not see Carlee nearly as often as he had. This increased Carlee's loneliness especially when she thought of the good times they had together and their true friendship.

When Walter's mind went to Carlee he deliberately resisted those romantic thoughts because he really did not want to let himself fall in love with her. He knew it could come to that if he let it. He kept his feelings platonic even in his thoughts. He was very proud of being an African-American man since his parents had given him the advantages of most affluent white men and he didn't want to disappoint their choices for the woman he chose to marry.

Carlee let him know that she had a sincere and deep friendship for him. She sincerely thought it could never be more than that because she couldn't even think of falling in love out of her race. Even mother realized that she was lonely for Walter's companionship and the cheerfulness that she maintained when they were together was now gradually slipping away. She seemed able to keep up with her school work which left her only one year of medical school which had been changed to a major in pediatrics the year before. As time went on though she seemed again to be approaching her old depressive state which made my parents very concerned. They had gone through it before so they insisted that she take a leave of absence from school and get back under father's friend's medical care. They felt she needed rest until she felt good again. She only had one year to go to complete medical school. Carlee also knew she needed to do this because of a severe weight loss caused by her loss of appetite.

Carlee planned to read the year's material that would normally be due if she had stayed in school. She also spent a lot of time with her baby girl Clare teaching her advanced subjects for small children. When Carlee came home, she would think of Walter but pushed any romantic ideas right out of her mind almost feeling like you would about a bad thought, and she would feel guilty. She did not yet tie it to my parents' attitude in raising her.

She was always so happy with both of them she couldn't seem to attach anything negative to them because both were so very good to her. Later in life I remembered Carlee telling me about one bad incident that she didn't forget.

Once when she was about ten, mother had an African-American housekeeper. She was a very nice woman named Jean and mother was very pleased with her housework. She had at least 5 children and mother would remember that and send little gifts or money whenever their birthdays came up, and Jean's as well.

Once Jean asked mother if Carlee could come home with her and meet her children in the future and come at different times to her house to play with them. She knew Carlee was alone most of the time at the house and she thought it would be a nice change for her. My mother knew that where Jean lived was not upscale but a nice old neighborhood. I could tell she was really nervous about it and said she had to discuss it with my father.

Not long after, when Jean left my mother's employment, although on good terms, I always wondered if it was because of that one incident. Other than that, Carlee was cherished by my parents, and the both of them did so many things to make her happy. Whatever ideas were apparent at her different age periods, they purchased those items which were toys to clothing and it was amazing how they kept up with it all especially at their age.

When Carlee came home, she was very lonely and especially missed Walter. She didn't realize it could be her hormones besides other things her doctor confided in her. She never had shared with him how much she had missed Walter since Walter went into his residency training. After a while Walter dropped by the school to see her and found out that she had taken a medical leave of absence from school. As soon as he found out he called her and let her know he was coming to see her in the next two days.

Mother was glad because she had heard from Carlee what a wonderful friend Walter was to her at school, and it was after he had left school that Carlee seemed to stay depressed. Her grandparents knew there was no romantic involvement between them but just a wonderful friendship. Mother noticed that almost immediately after he called that Carlee began to perk up and get things ready for his coming. When he came to the door Carlee greeted him and introduced him to her grandmother.

Mother couldn't help but think what a fine looking African-American man he was with a beautiful sports car he had parked outside. He also had the warmest smile, and wonderful personality. When Carlee saw him she just hugged him as if there was a piece of her missing. He asked her grandmother if he could take her out for a ride. From their past together he knew she loved rides in the country. As a gentleman, he let her grandmother know where they were going and let her know what time he would have her home. When they got in the car Carlee said she never knew how much she missed him until he came to the door that day. He said he had to admit he felt the same way about her. She asked him if he had gotten serious with some of his girlfriends that she had met, but he admitted he had not.

Before they arrived at our home, he told her he would be coming to take her on these small trips that both of them had liked so much in the past, until he felt that she was again getting better on her own, and to this she agreed heartily. As he drove he talked about his residency and let her know he was going to establish his practice in the state where they were living.

He was sincerely hoping to keep up with their visitations because he did not want to stop seeing her as he had after graduation. Carlee was so happy to hear this. When they both arrived at home, Walter met Carlee's grandfather and explained his motives for coming to see her. My father could see what a fine young man he was and was glad to know that he would be visiting her again especially since he knew they had been such good friends and he could see the change in her already. She was radiant when her grandfather came home from work. Walter also met baby Clare and she warmed right up to him.

Father talked a little bit about Walter's father's football career and let him know he had been to some of his games. He explained to Walter that Carlee's doctor had told him that Carlee had a broken heart and until it was mended she would slip back into these depressive episodes. Because of his clinical training Walter realized the same thing about Carlee but he knew she could come out of it. He was sorry that he had to leave her for a time but he would do his best to make his visits as frequent as he could.

He explained how close they had become the two years she was in medical school with him and now he was able to fit her into some of the slots of his residency program. Because of this he could see her much more often and as a patient. My father agreed remembering what a friend Jenifer was to Clare and how close he and mother had come to her family. My father still didn't know the main reason that Carlee's husband left her. It was because of that promise she had made to Joe thinking that in time it would work itself out. But as time went on his rejection took a real toll on her which she couldn't share with her grandparents. After talking with Walter, her grandfather agreed with him and gave him permission to spend the needed time with Carlee.

So a least twice a week he would visit her and take her places that he knew would cheer her up and make her feel she was really cared for. Within weeks Carlee's grandmother and grandfather could see the wonderful change in her and what a fine man Walter was. Carlee blossomed like a rose. One incident that she shared with my parents was that on one of their trips, Walter had to stop by his house to drop off a package for his mother.

As they were driving down this long road to the house which was in the best part of that community, they turned off on what Carlee thought was a street, and after driving in about three blocks, she saw this gorgeous mansion and Walter drove up to the door. He got out, hastened into the house leaving her in the car. The mother noticed this and insisted that he bring Carlee inside. The mansion was beautiful and all of Carlee's families' houses paled against this mansion inside and out. There was a pool, tennis court, basketball court, manicured shrubbery and a beautiful fountain in front of the house.

When she got inside and was introduced, his mother mentioned that Walter shared some lovely descriptions of her, especially of her beautiful blue eyes. And when she met her she wanted to give her a pin that she had gotten abroad that matched her eyes since he was so enamored with them. Carlee sensed after receiving the pin, that his mother was a lovely caring woman. She and Walter had to leave right away because the trip to his house had cut off some of the time he could spend with her that day.

The doctor friend became close to Walter and they became good friends and they compared their diagnosis of her problem. Like the doctor, Walter realized that some of the problem was hormonal. With all these facts coming together and the closeness between them, Carlee talked with Walter admitting to him that she had never thought more about him than being a wonderful friend. This was because of the prejudice she was raised with, and yet she couldn't find any fault with him and he certainly was a better man than her husband in every way. She also told him that he never gave her a reason to reach out to him other than in friendship and if he had, she would have been cured earlier of her husband's rejection.

She always felt cared for by Walter but not in a romantic way and that was what she needed but even she didn't realize it at the time. My parents saw a change in her within weeks and also continued to see what a fine man Walter was. She then talked to her grandfather about him when she realized it was her upbringing that had put these prejudiced feelings inside of her. To want him for more than a good friend was impossible. If he had tried to come close to her romantically she may have overcome this hurdle but he never did even though she always knew he sincerely cared about her. Carlee explained to her grandfather that as time went on she realized that she was falling in love with Walter and her feelings for him were growing stronger than what she thought she could do about it. On one of their outings she broke down and told Walter what she had discovered in their relationship. She knew now it was more than friendship and for her it was love. He wasn't shocked because recently he had been holding back this feeling of love that he had for her. After they brought it to the light, they knew they had to straighten this out with her grandparents and his parents.

To Carlee's surprise my parents could see that this fine man was the right man for Carlee even though neither one planned it this way. They also admitted that though it took years for them to realize it, they had exposed their children and now their grandchildren to their bigotries, and had only begun to open their eyes in these later years of their lives. If they had not moved north they would have never realized it. After Carlee poured out her feelings to her grandparents they realized how much Walter had true love for her. They spoke to him telling him they could lay their feelings aside and accept him as part of their family still not knowing that Carlee actually had African- American blood in her.

My parents were already near retirement and had planned to move back to the South but now they had to give that some thought especially having Carlee's wedding to Walter just a head of their retirement. Carlee did not want a large wedding like she had with Joe but would rather use those funds to finish school and to develop her practice after graduation.

As soon as I heard about the wedding I was able to gently explain to Carlee and my parents what had happened in the family, first with Clare, and then with Carlee, Carlee's Dad, and now baby Clare.

Chapter 8

"THE WEDDING"

Learning all this was a shock but a good shock because it brought the family together, and when they realized that African-American blood had come into the family, mother told Jenifer's mother June and they laughed over it, which brought us all even closer.

The wedding was small and very nice with just the family and very close friends. However, before the wedding Carlee thought of including Joe since Clare had never met her father. She decided to get in touch with Joe very discreetly now that she had found out where he was living. She discussed this first with Walter, then with her grandparents, and they gave their blessing for her to get in touch with him, also because so much in the family had been cleared up.

When Joe heard from her, instead of being cold and distant, he was so glad to hear from her and that she was marrying again. He also wanted to see her and bring his new wife and family so that they could meet Clare. He explained that God had used his wife after he had told her about his daughter to show him how wrong he had been with his racist attitude. Because she had grown up with parents who had recognized when she was very young that they were wrong in their prejudice, and from then on they raised her not to harbor those feelings.

Joe admitted that the change did not happen to him immediately; but with the changes that came through the Civil Rights Movement and his wife not wanting their children growing up with hateful racist attitudes that he had, he finally realized that he had to change. He had often thought of Clare and what a beautiful baby he gave up but that didn't come until later when his two children were born with blond hair and blue eyes, like Clare. He realized as his doctor friend had told him that it was very unlikely that what that nurse saw would have never shown up, and he missed out on those early years of raising his daughter. Now he knows because of his wife that even if it did show up, that Clare was still his child and he wanted her to know it and have her spend time with him and his new family. He knew Clare had had a brand new father in Walter and he along with Carlee were medical doctors.

Joe and his family attended Carlee's wedding. Everyone got along with everyone and especially with Walter when Joe heard who his football player father was. All was forgiven. Clare met her father even though she did not fully understand who he was because Walter had become her father in the months that Carlee was preparing for the wedding. Joe, by this time was very wealthy and could afford to stay with his family in the most beautiful and best hotel in the city. After the wedding he and his wife wanted to stay several more days so from the hotel they dropped in on the family and also toured the area where they were staying which was a famous tourist area with lots of sights and exclusive tours sponsored by the hotel.

Joe also remembered meeting Hugh, and promised to look him up when he returned home. His wife fit right in with the family along with the children and they were so glad they had come and gained these new relatives. Joe let Carlee know that his father had passed away but like Joe he had made a change and repented of the way he had thought all those years and the negative influence he had on his children.

Walter and Carlee had a wonderful honeymoon that was paid for by his parents. Since his mother and father traveled abroad a lot they picked out very unusual places for them to visit in Europe. These places were the usual and the very unusual. Their honeymoon lasted three whole weeks with my parents babysitting Clare. When they returned home, they worked on their practices and decided to combine them even though they were different.

They now had two built-in grandmothers, my mother and Walter's mother. This gave both of them personal time with their husbands and time with

Clare. Of course as time went on, Carlee and Walter had two more children so my parents weren't going abroad so often and they loved it. The whole family attended different churches but serving the same Lord.

Conclusion

$\mathcal{J}$oe and his family joined the family on many vacations and the children even attended several colleges together because they had become so close.

My husband and I had three children, and we have had a wonderful life thanks to the openness of that Quaker School. I was able to adjust to most of the challenges in my life because of it and because of Jenifer's mother's influence.

I got more serious about my faith and we joined a church with real Christian values so our children grew up without prejudice and my husband adjusted well to these new truths. Hugh's wife knew about his African-American mother for years and blended right in with all the members of our family during vacations and special occasions. All the children loved each other and got along well going on vacation together and visiting each other at our homes.

When my parents passed away in their 80's their estate provided a good income for my husband and me, and all of their grandchildren had trust funds set up by my father. And now the secret is out at last to this generation and we are all doing well because of it.

The End

About the Author

$\mathcal{J}$anice Freeman was born in New York City in the Bronx in 1936. She was the daughter of Ben and Mattye Watson and she grew up with two older brothers.

They moved from New York when she was eleven to a lovely community in New Jersey, and the three children finished a very fine high school there. Because of her high school education she learned to read and love novels, many of which were classical works. This reading opened her up to a love for good films and other classical genre.

When she finished college she married and went into a career never thinking about writing. She later became a Pastor in her life and was into that area until she was 70 years old and she then retired.

Because she wanted to do more with her life by the time she was 80, she thought of writing a book that would show a different side of the effects of segregation on white life in America and through the Family Secret came this idea.